STEM *trailblazer* BIOS

VACCINE INNOVATORS

PEARL KENDRICK AND GRACE ELDERING

S. WOOD

Lerner Publications ◆ Minneapolis

Lerner Publications Company
A division of Lerner Publishing Group, Inc.
241 First Avenue North
Minneapolis, MN 55401 U.S.A.

For reading levels and more information, look up this title at www.lernerbooks.com.

Content Consultant: Carolyn G. Shapiro-Shapin, PhD, Professor of History, Grand Valley State University

Library of Congress Cataloging-in-Publication Data

Names: Wood, Susan, 1965– author.
Title: Vaccine innovators Pearl Kendrick and Grace Eldering / by S. Wood.
Other titles: STEM trailblazer bios.
Description: Minneapolis : Lerner Publications, [2017] | Series: STEM trailblazer bios | Includes bibliographical references and index.
Identifiers: LCCN 2016008856 (print) | LCCN 2016012516 (ebook) | ISBN 9781512407907 (lb : alk. paper) | ISBN 9781512413076 (pb : alk. paper) | ISBN 9781512410938 (eb pdf)
Subjects: LCSH: Kendrick, Pearl, 1890–1980—Juvenile literature. | Eldering, Grace, 1900–1988—Juvenile literature. | Women bacteriologists—Biography—Juvenile literature. | Bacteriologists—Biography—Juvenile literature. | Pertussis vaccines—History—Juvenile literature. | Whooping cough—History—Juvenile literature. | Discoveries in science—Juvenile literature.
Classification: LCC QR30 .W66 2017 (print) | LCC QR30 (ebook) | DDC 579.30922—dc23

LC record available at http://lccn.loc.gov/2016008856

Manufactured in the United States of America
1 – PC – 7/15/16

The images in this book are used with the permission of: © Daily Mail/Rex/Alamy Stock Photo, pp. 4, 26; Public Domain, p. 5; Library of Congress, pp. 6 (LC-USZ62-106940), 22 (LC-USZ62-25812); © ggw1962/Shutterstock.com, p. 8; © Everett Historical/Shutterstock.com, p. 10; © Dr. M.A. Ansary/Science Source, p. 11; © Asianet-Pakistan/Shutterstock.com, p. 12; © Duncan Smith/Stockbyte/Thinkstock, p. 14; © Pearl L. Kendrick papers, 1888-1979/Bentley Historical Library, University of Michigan, p. 16; © J.L. Carson Custom Medical Stock Photo/Newscom, p. 18; © Chris Ware/ZumaPress/Newscom, p. 20; © World History Archive/Alamy Stock Photo, p. 23; © Grand Rapids History and Special Collections, Archives, Grand Rapids Public Library, Grand Rapids, Michigan, p. 25; © Justin Sullivan/Getty Images News/Thinkstock, p. 28.

Front Cover: © Grand Rapids History and Special Collections, Archives, Grand Rapids Public Library, Grand Rapids, Michigan.

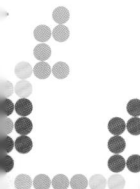

CONTENTS

Chapter 1

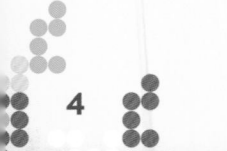

A nurse sits with a group of sick children who may have whooping cough.

BECOMING SCIENTISTS

When Pearl Kendrick and Grace Eldering were very young, they both got sick with whooping cough. Whooping cough makes children cough until they are out of breath. The disease can be deadly. Pearl and Grace were lucky to survive.

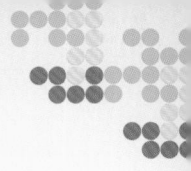

A LOVE OF SCIENCE

Pearl Kendrick was born on August 24, 1890, in Wheaton, Illinois. Pearl's father was a minister. Whenever he moved to a new church, Pearl and her family went with him. She grew up mostly in New York.

Pearl was an excellent student. When Pearl was a young woman, she had questions about evolution. Evolution is the idea that living things change and adapt over many generations. To find answers to her questions, Pearl went to Syracuse University. She studied zoology, or the science of animals. She graduated in 1914. Later, Pearl became a teacher and a principal.

Pearl's first love was science. She wanted to learn more. So in the summer of 1917, she enrolled at Columbia University.

Lyman Hall was home to the Syracuse University zoology department.

A woman operates a tool-manufacturing machine at a Massachusetts factory during World War I. Women took over jobs in many industries during the war.

She studied **bacteriology**. She was hired in 1919 by the New York State Department of Health as a laboratory assistant. Now Pearl was working full time as a scientist.

It was a good time for women to enter science. Many men were off fighting in World War I (1914–1918). This left openings for women in new scientific fields. In 1920, the head of the Michigan Department of Health hired Kendrick to work at a laboratory in Lansing. He promised Kendrick she could advance her career as a scientist.

He was right. In 1926, Kendrick became the head of a state health lab in Grand Rapids, Michigan. At the lab, Kendrick and her coworkers did tests to study diseases. They also tested milk and water for harmful organisms. They made sure the liquids were safe for people to drink.

The state health department believed in education for its workers. It gave workers funds and time off to further their studies. In 1932 Kendrick earned an advanced degree in bacteriology from Johns Hopkins University. It was a Doctor of Science degree. Now she was Dr. Pearl Kendrick.

Kendrick continued to work at the state health lab in Grand Rapids. There, Kendrick met another scientist. Together, they would create a lifesaving vaccine.

The Michigan Department of Health tested water and milk for bacteria. These bacteria could make people very sick.

FROM VOLUNTEER TO SCIENTIST

That other scientist was Grace Eldering. Grace was born on September 5, 1900, in Myers, Montana. She grew up in the small town of Rancher, Montana, on the Yellowstone River. As a young person, Grace wanted to become a doctor. She studied biology and chemistry at the University of Montana, but she needed more education to become a doctor. For a time, Grace taught English because she did not have enough money to continue her schooling.

Grace heard about a program at the Michigan Department of Health. Volunteers could work for no pay as they trained to become lab workers. It seemed to be a good way to start a science career. Grace traveled to Michigan. She joined the volunteer training program and was soon hired as a lab worker. In 1932 Grace was moved to the lab in Grand Rapids to help with milk and water testing. There, she joined Pearl Kendrick's staff. Thanks to the department's educational program, Grace later earned her Doctor of Science degree from Johns Hopkins University in 1941.

TECH TALK

"I always knew . . . that if a woman worked in a field that was largely occupied by men . . . she had to be a little bit better."

—Grace Eldering, on working in a male-dominated field

Chapter 2

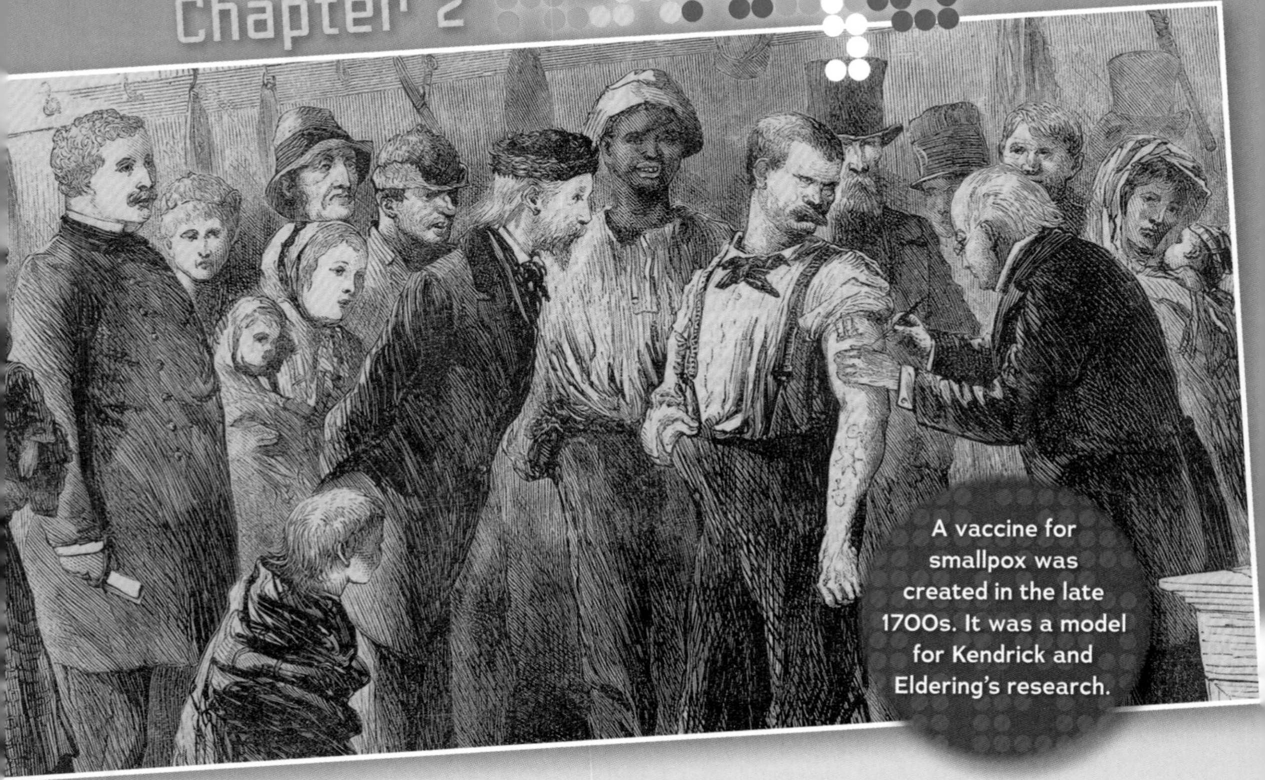

A vaccine for smallpox was created in the late 1700s. It was a model for Kendrick and Eldering's research.

DANGEROUS DISEASE

In 1932 whooping cough was sweeping through Grand Rapids. Children were getting very sick. Kendrick and Eldering wanted to create a whooping cough vaccine. Vaccines prevent people from getting sick. Scientists had created vaccines for other diseases, but not yet for whooping cough.

WHAT IS WHOOPING COUGH?

This illness causes long, violent coughing. The cough is followed by a "whoop" sound as the sick person tries to catch his or her breath. Sometimes children cough so hard they throw up. It can take weeks to get better.

Whooping cough is very **contagious**. When people who have the disease cough or sneeze, they can spread the whooping cough bacteria to others. By the 1920s, approximately six thousand US children were dying every year from the illness.

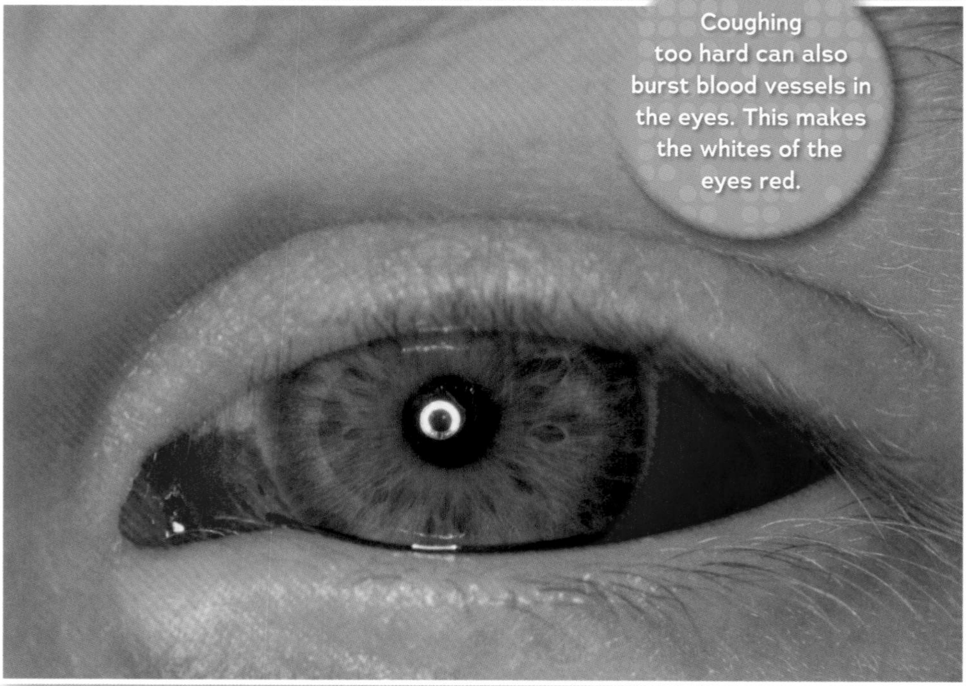

Coughing too hard can also burst blood vessels in the eyes. This makes the whites of the eyes red.

Kendrick and Eldering wanted to create a vaccine to stop whooping cough. Vaccines use the body's natural ability to fight disease. Harmful organisms, such as bacteria, cause many diseases. A vaccine places a safe version of a harmful organism into the body. The body learns how to fight the harmful organism. The body then remembers how to protect itself from that organism. This protection is called immunity.

Vaccines come in different forms. Some you take by mouth. Others are sprayed in your nose. Some are shots you may get in your arm.

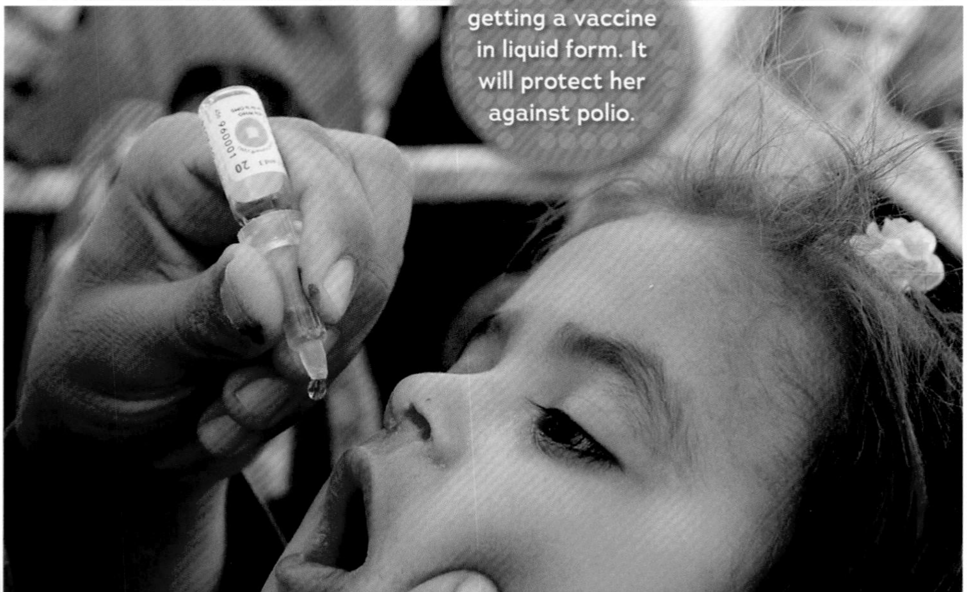

This girl is getting a vaccine in liquid form. It will protect her against polio.

TECH TALK

"When the work day was over, we started on the research because it was fun. We'd come home, feed the dogs, get some dinner, and get back to what was interesting."

—Pearl Kendrick, on the early stages of the vaccine research

Kendrick and Eldering received permission to work on a whooping cough vaccine at the Michigan state lab. But they could work on it only after their daily duties were done. This was similar to taking on another job without extra pay. But the scientists were excited by their vaccine research.

Chapter 3

A type of bacteria called *Bordetella pertussis* causes whooping cough. The disease is also called pertussis.

THE WORK BEGINS

Kendrick and Eldering needed samples of whooping cough bacteria to study at the lab. They asked local doctors and nurses to collect samples. Sick children coughed onto a small glass dish called a "cough plate." The bacteria from their coughs lived in **growth media** inside the dish. The substance fed the bacteria so it would grow.

Kendrick and Eldering stored the cough plates at the lab. Using microscopes, the scientists studied the bacteria on the cough plates.

THE COST OF WHOOPING COUGH

Kendrick and Eldering also gathered samples themselves. They visited sick children in their homes. Many families the scientists saw were very poor. They lived in small, crowded apartments. The country was in the grip of the Great Depression. The

TECH TALK

"We learned about the disease and the Depression at the same time. . . . We listened to sad stories told by desperate fathers who could find no work. We collected specimens by the light of [oil] lamps, from whooping . . . strangling children. We saw what the disease could do."

—Grace Eldering, on collecting bacteria for vaccine research

Pearl Kendrick studies a whooping cough sample in her laboratory.

US economy had failed in 1929, causing many companies and banks to close. Many people lost their jobs or savings.

Whooping cough made some families even poorer. Children with whooping cough were often quarantined. The sick person had to stay at home, away from others, so the illness would not spread. Sometimes the sick child's whole family had to stay home. This meant parents could not go to their jobs. Sometimes they had to miss several weeks of work with no pay.

QUARANTINE VICTORY

At the lab, Kendrick, Eldering, and other staff scientists learned all they could about whooping cough. They studied the cough plates and watched how the bacteria grew. They asked the same sick children to cough on more plates. If bacteria grew on the new plates, then the children were still contagious. If no bacteria grew, then the children could no longer spread the disease. In this way, the scientists learned exactly how long a person with whooping cough is contagious.

Kendrick and Eldering shared what they learned with the Grand Rapids Health Department. The health department created more precise quarantine rules. This change was a victory, but Kendrick and Eldering's work had just begun.

Chapter 4

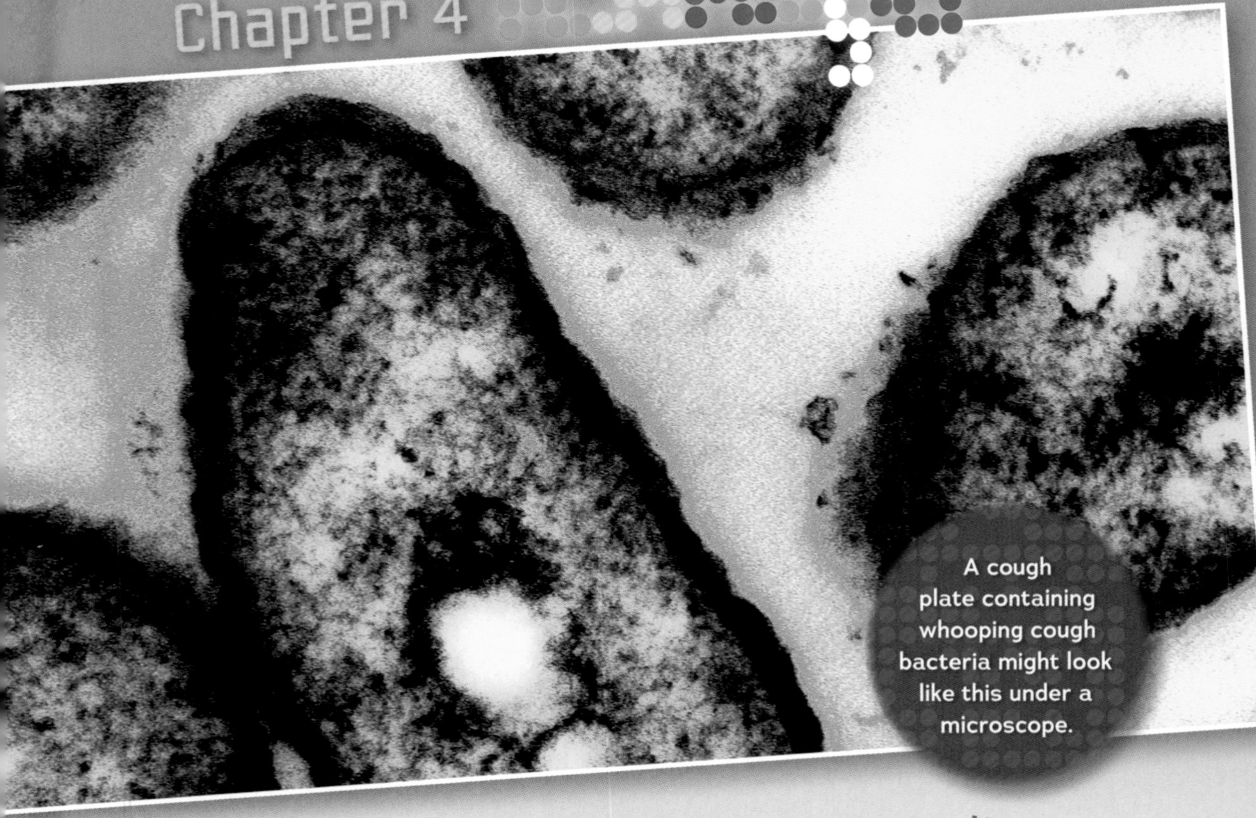

A cough plate containing whooping cough bacteria might look like this under a microscope.

DEVELOPING THE VACCINE

Kendrick and Eldering had learned a lot about whooping cough. Now they could begin making a vaccine. They decided their vaccine should contain dead whooping cough bacteria. This meant the vaccine could not cause the disease. It would only activate immunity.

The scientists went to work. They washed live bacteria off the cough plates and into a salt solution. They killed the bacteria with chemicals and cold temperatures. The result was a vaccine.

The scientists tested the vaccine for safety. They wanted to be sure the amount of dead bacteria was not harmful. They also confirmed other organisms had not entered the vaccine as it was being made.

The scientists injected mice, guinea pigs, and rabbits with the vaccine. The animals showed no ill effects. To be certain the vaccine was safe, Kendrick and Eldering even injected themselves. They, too, had no ill effects.

At last, Kendrick and Eldering had their whooping cough vaccine. But how could they be certain it worked?

THE FIRST TRIAL

Kendrick and Eldering needed to try the vaccine on children and record the results. Scientists call this a trial. Children getting the vaccine would be the trial's **test group**. Kendrick and Eldering also needed a **control group**. Children not getting the vaccine would be the trial's control group. The scientists could then compare the results between the two groups.

At that time, some researchers used **orphans** for their

Kids spent a lot of time together in school. This made it hard to isolate sick kids before whooping cough spread.

tests. Those researchers did not have to ask permission from parents to run their tests. But many people believed this practice was unfair to orphans. Kendrick and Eldering chose not to use orphans for their research.

Once again, the scientists looked to their community. They worked with area doctors and nurses, parent–teacher groups, women's groups, and the health department to build support for the trial. Parents across Grand Rapids let their children take part. Many were eager to help. The parents understood that Kendrick and Eldering's vaccine was important. They knew it might put an end to a deadly childhood disease.

ENCOURAGING RESULTS

The trial's results were exciting. The test group was made up of 712 children who received the vaccine. Only four developed mild cases of whooping cough. The control group was made up of 880 children who did not receive the vaccine. Of those, forty-five children developed severe cases of whooping cough.

It appeared as if Kendrick and Eldering's vaccine had stopped children from getting whooping cough. But the scientists needed to be sure.

TECH TALK

"Perhaps the most interesting fact [from the trial] was the demonstration of what can be accomplished by a whole community working together."

—Grace Eldering, on the trial testing of the whooping cough vaccine

Chapter 5

Eleanor Roosevelt was passionate about disease prevention.

SAVING LIVES

The first vaccine trial was a success. But Kendrick and Eldering wanted to expand their study and test a larger group. However, money for their research was running low. The scientists needed funds for staff and supplies. So Kendrick invited First Lady Eleanor Roosevelt to visit the lab. Maybe the first lady could help. After all, she shared the scientists' interests in keeping the children healthy.

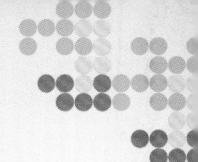

Roosevelt cared about treatments for childhood diseases. Her husband, President Franklin Roosevelt, had **polio**. The first lady was also troubled by the use of orphans for research. She had asked the government to look into it.

Polio, a dangerous disease, affected Franklin D. Roosevelt's legs. It was hard for him to walk without assistance.

Roosevelt toured Kendrick and Eldering's lab in 1936. There, she learned about the scientists' work. She was impressed by their ethics and their progress on the vaccine. Roosevelt found money for more lab staff.

THE SECOND TRIAL

With more funding for their lab, Kendrick and Eldering launched a second, larger trial. More than four thousand children were involved. The scientists compared the results from the test group and the control group. Again, the trial was a success. The results proved that the vaccine worked. So the Michigan Department of Health began making the whooping cough vaccine for all of its citizens. Soon the vaccine was being used across the United States.

Kendrick and Eldering continued to study whooping cough. In the 1940s, Kendrick asked scientist Loney Clinton Gordon to join her team. Gordon, an African American woman, developed better growth media for whooping cough bacteria. She also discovered a type of whooping cough bacteria that was stronger than others. Using those stronger bacteria, the scientists were able to make the vaccine even more powerful.

Over the years, the number of whooping cough cases decreased significantly. In 1934, before the vaccine, there

Loney Gordon (*left*) and Eldering (*third from right*) meet with other members of the research team.

were 209 cases of the disease for every 100,000 Americans. After 1960, there were fewer than 10 cases per 100,000 Americans. That was a huge drop. Many lives were saved.

But Kendrick and Eldering were not finished. They had a new project in mind. They knew children did not enjoy shots,

Kendrick explains the whooping cough vaccine during a visit to a laboratory.

even though they were necessary. The scientists wanted to combine multiple vaccines, including the one against whooping cough, into a single shot. The combination vaccine, called Tdap and based on Kendrick and Eldering's work, is still in use more than seventy years later.

Kendrick and Eldering shared their research with scientists around the world. Scientists from other nations visited the lab in Michigan. Kendrick traveled a lot after her and Eldering's success. She helped with vaccine programs in the United Kingdom, Mexico, Eastern Europe, and Central and South America. She later went to work at the University of Michigan. Eldering then took over the lab.

TECH TALK

"Who are the men and women living today who would be dead from whooping cough had it not been for [Kendrick and Eldering's] vaccine? We can conclude . . . that several hundred thousand of them are now leading productive lives, in this country alone."

—Dean Richard Remington, University of Michigan School of Public Health

Kendrick and Eldering never looked for praise for their whooping cough vaccine. They rarely talked about themselves in public. And they never claimed all the credit. They felt they could not have created the vaccine without the aid of many people. This included the thousands of children who took part in their trials and helped with their research. Ultimately, Kendrick and Eldering's hard work saved many lives.

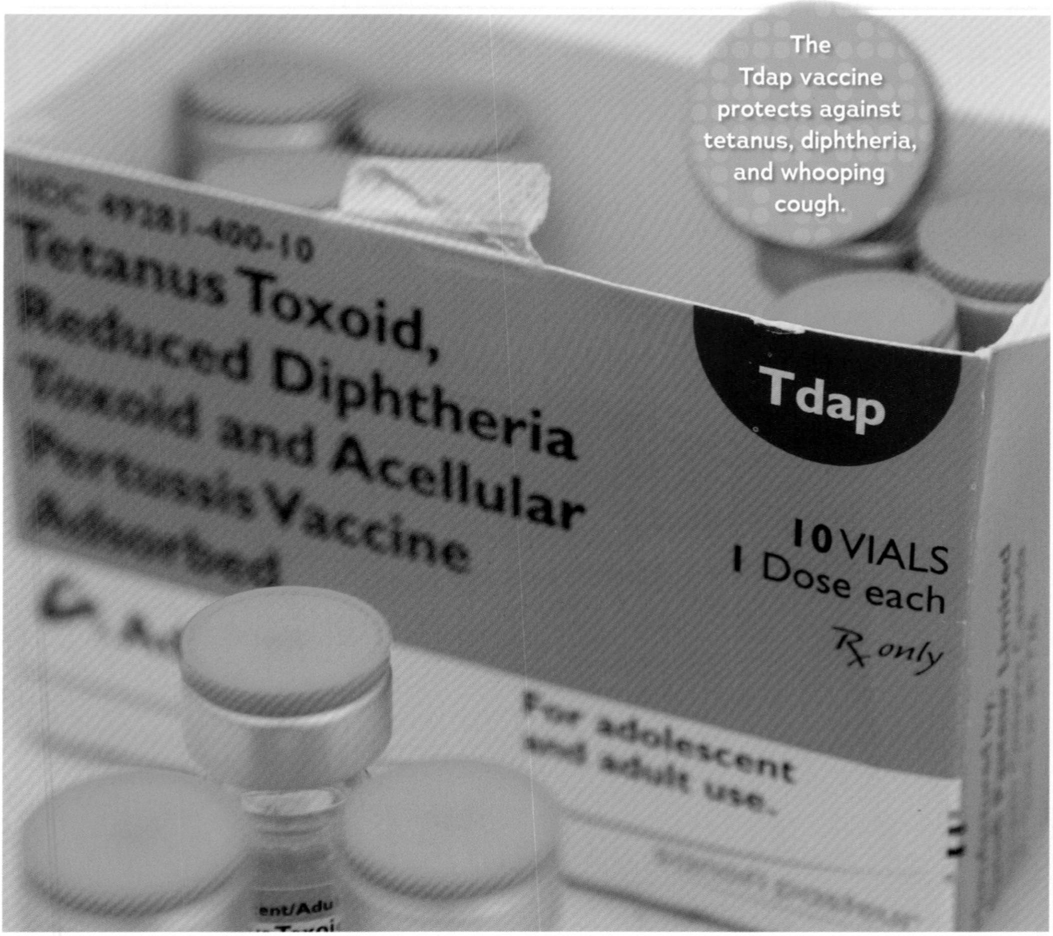

The Tdap vaccine protects against tetanus, diphtheria, and whooping cough.

TIMELINE

1890

Pearl Kendrick is born on August 24 in Wheaton, Illinois.

1900

Grace Eldering is born on September 5 in Myers, Montana.

1914

World War I begins.

1926

Kendrick becomes head of the state health lab in Grand Rapids, Michigan.

1929

The US economy fails and the Great Depression begins.

1932

Eldering comes to work at Kendrick's lab in Grand Rapids. They decide to work together on a whooping cough vaccine.

1934

The first vaccine trial begins. Results show the vaccine seems to work.

1936

First Lady Eleanor Roosevelt visits Kendrick and Eldering's lab.

1938

The second, larger vaccine trial begins. Results prove the vaccine works.

1940

Kendrick and Eldering's whooping cough vaccine is used across the United States. There are far fewer cases of the disease. The vaccine saves many lives around the world.

SOURCE NOTES

9 Virginia Law Burns, *Bold Women in Michigan History* (Missoula, MT: Mountain Press, 2006), 72.

13 Carolyn G. Shapiro-Shapin, "'A Whole Community Working Together': Pearl Kendrick, Grace Eldering, and the Grand Rapids Pertussis Trials, 1932–1939." *Michigan Historical Review* 33.1 (2007): 67.

15 Harry M. Marks, "The Kendrick-Eldering-(Frost) Pertussis Vaccine Field Trial," *Journal of the Royal Society of Medicine* 100.5 (2007): 243.

21 Carolyn G. Shapiro-Shapin, "'A Whole Community Working Together,'" 85.

27 Carolyn G. Shapiro-Shapin, "Pearl Kendrick, Grace Eldering, and the Pertussis Vaccine," *Emerging Infectious Diseases* 16. 8 (2010): 1277.

GLOSSARY

bacteriology
the study of bacteria

contagious
easily spread

control group
in a scientific trial, the group not getting the test

growth media
a substance that feeds bacteria so it will grow and can be studied

orphans
children whose parents are no longer living

polio
a disease often developed in childhood that causes nerve damage

test group
in a scientific trial, the group getting the test

FURTHER INFORMATION

BOOKS

Allman, Toney. *Whooping Cough*. Detroit: Lucent Books, 2012. Read more about how the whooping cough affects the body.

Hand, Carol. *Vaccines*. Minneapolis, MN: Abdo, 2014. Follow the development of vaccines and how they have changed.

Smith, Linda Wasmer. *Louis Pasteur: Genius Disease Fighter*. Berkeley Heights, NJ: Enslow, 2015. Learn more about another scientist who fought diseases using vaccines and other methods.

WEBSITES

Michigan Women's Hall of Fame

http://www.michiganwomenshalloffame.org/inductees_by_name.aspx

Read more about scientists Pearl Kendrick, Grace Eldering, and Loney Clinton Gordon.

Science Heroes: Grace Eldering

http://scienceheroes.com/index.php?option=com_content&view=article&id=156&Itemid=155

Discover how Grace Eldering's work led to a lifesaving vaccine.

Science Heroes: Pearl Kendrick

http://scienceheroes.com/index.php?option=com_content&view=article&id=167&Itemid=166

Learn more about Pearl Kendrick's work.

INDEX

ABOUT THE AUTHOR

S. Wood is an author of nonfiction for young readers and adults. She specializes in biography because she enjoys telling the stories of people's lives, adventures, and accomplishments. She makes her home in Virginia.